THE SONS OF KORAH

THE SONS OF KORAH

Stephen Kaung

Christian Fellowship Publishers, Inc.
New York

Paperback ISBN: 978-1-68062-125-9
eBook ISBN: 978-1-68062-126-6

Available from the Publishers at:

11515 Allecingie Parkway
Richmond, Virginia 23235
www. c-f-p.com

Printed in the United States of America

Preface

Of the one hundred and fifty Psalms, there are twelve attributed to the sons of Korah. They were special Psalms to be sung by special people. The mercy of God had spared them from the destruction that their ancestor Korah had deserved (see Numbers 16). They went through death and out of death into resurrection life. They became the children of mercy and grace—sons of the cross. Through this experience of the cross, they appreciated God uniquely and were called to be the doorkeepers and singers in His temple. They dedicated themselves to God in a living way. Out of the abundance of their hearts, they could sing these songs to God.

In this volume, four of these Psalms are considered in detail along with their main themes of:

HOPE—Psalm 42 (43),
FAITH—Psalm 44,
LOVE—Psalm 45, and
VICTORY—Psalm 46.

These *sons of the cross* could sing from the fullness of their hearts and out of their experience. As we too have received the mercy of God, may our hearts also overflow with worship and praise as we consider these Psalms of the sons of Korah.

Contents

Unless otherwise indicated,
Scripture quotations are from the
New Translation by J. N. Darby.

1—Psalm 42: Hope

Psalm 42—To the chief Musician.
An instruction; of the sons of Korah.

As the hart panteth after the water-brooks, so panteth my soul after thee, O God.

My soul thirsteth for God, for the living God: when shall I come and appear before God?

My tears have been my bread day and night, while they say unto me all the day, Where is thy God?

These things I remember and have poured out my soul within me: how I passed along with the multitude, how I went on with them to the house of God, with the voice of joy and praise, a festive multitude.

Why art thou cast down, my soul, and art disquieted in me? hope in God; for I shall yet praise him, for the health of his countenance.

My God, my soul is cast down within me; therefore do I remember thee from the land of the Jordan, and the Hermons, from mount Mizar.

Deep calleth unto deep at the noise of thy cataracts; all thy breakers and thy billows are gone over me.

> In the day-time will Jehovah command his loving-kindness, and in the night his song shall be with me, a prayer unto the God of my life.
>
> I will say unto God my rock, Why hast thou forgotten me? why go I mourning because of the oppression of the enemy?
>
> As with a crushing in my bones mine adversaries reproach me, while they say unto me all the day, Where is thy God?
>
> Why art thou cast down, my soul? and why art thou disquieted within me? hope in God; for I shall yet praise him, who is the health of my countenance, and my God.

Of the one hundred and fifty psalms, there are twelve attributed to the sons of Korah. Who are these sons? Back in Numbers 16, there was a rebellion among the children of Israel, which was headed by a man called Korah. He was a Kohite of the tribe of Levi and was given the high privilege of serving in the tabernacle. Yet, he led a great rebellion not only against Moses and Aaron but against God himself. Korah, Dathan, and Abiram of the tribe of Reuben, and two hundred and fifty leaders of the congregation of Israel, rebelled against God's order. They came to Moses and Aaron and said:

> It is enough; for all the assembly, all of them are holy, and Jehovah is among them; and why do ye

> lift up yourselves above the congregation of Jehovah? (Numbers 16:3).

Outwardly it seemed to be a very spiritual protest, but if you read the chapter, you will find Moses pointed out to Korah that God had given him a great privilege in serving the tabernacle. Why did he desire the priesthood which God had desired for the sons of Aaron? He also reproached Dathan and Abiram and asked them why they rebelled against God.

Out of that great rebellion, God did a new thing. The earth was opened, and Korah, Dathan, and Abiram, and those that belonged to them, were swallowed into Hades alive. As the two hundred and fifty leaders were trying to offer incense to God, they were burned to death. This was the man Korah. But isn't it strange that the sons of Korah became the sweet singers of Israel?

The children of Korah were spared. "But the children of Korah died not" (Numbers 26:11). They did not die with their father. We do not know whether these sons participated in the conspiracy with their father or not; but, they repented. These children of Korah passed through great affliction. They saw their father literally swallowed by the earth and saw the people burned to death, yet they were spared. With fear and trembling, they realized it was only by the mercy of God that they were not consumed. Because of that, they offered themselves to God in a way that seemed to be higher than many other people. They were the sons of the cross and had passed through the sufferings of the cross. They had gone through death and out of death into resurrection life. They were surely the children of the mercy and grace of God. Being touched by God's mercy and grace in sparing them, they dedicated themselves to God in a very living and real way.

If you read I and II Chronicles, you will see they became not only the doorkeepers of the tabernacle but also the singers in the house of God. Out of their deep experience, they became the doorkeepers. In other words, they knew who could enter into the house of God and serve and who could not. They knew who could approach the altar and who could not. It was not a theory to them but experience, and because of that, they were fit for that kind of service. Out of their deep experience, they knew how to sing unto the Lord. They were not professional singers as we might think, but they knew how to sing unto the Lord a new song. They continued even to the days of Hezekiah. These were the sons of Korah.

In the reading of these eleven or twelve Psalms, we find expressions of deep affliction, trouble, problems, death, and persecutions; but, we also see that out of them come forth hope, faith, and love. Their only desire was for the living God. So I do believe in these psalms of the sons of Korah there are spiritual and eternal lessons for us to learn so that we, like them, may have songs to sing unto our God.

of the sons of Korah

Or it may read, "…for the sons of Korah." We do not know if this means the sons of Korah composed these Psalms. We believe that most of the Psalms were composed by David. C. H. Spurgeon entitles the one hundred and fifty Psalms as *The Treasury of David*. Even though there is no mention of David's name in some Psalms, as the sweet singer of Israel, we can find him there. Most likely, the greater part of these Psalms was written by David—a man after God's own heart, a man who had gone through so much, been on mountain tops, in deep valleys, passed through the valley of the shadow of death, and been on the rock, the tower, the high place. Out of his manifold experiences of God, he poured out his heart in Psalms to sing unto God.

Probably David wrote the Psalms, gave them to the chief Musician to be put to music, and the sons of Korah sang them in the house of God. It is not just for anyone to sing Psalms unto God; it requires a certain spiritual history, background, and experience to enter into the spirit of David and the spirit of Christ. The sons of Korah were qualified to sing these songs. May the Lord help us—though we may not be the ones who compose these Psalms—that by His mercy we might have a taste of what David and the other saints have gone through, and out of these experiences, we will be qualified to sing these songs and be accepted.

An instruction

Psalm 42 is the first of these Psalms of the sons of Korah. It is an instruction—an instruction ode. This Psalm is to teach and instruct us in the things of God. It has a permanent and eternal value, and it is something which we ought to learn by heart.

Most commentators believe that the background for this Psalm was the time when Absalom, David's son, rebelled against him (see II Samuel 15). Absalom was able to gather the people against his father, and David, being in such danger, had to flee from Jerusalem in haste. A number of people fled with him. As they went over Mount Olive, David had his head covered, his feet bare, and he was weeping. The people who were with him covered their heads also as they were in such shame and reproach. The priests who bore the ark of God came to David to flee with him, but he told them to go back to Jerusalem to the tent which was set for the ark; because if God should show mercy to him, he would come back.

As he went over the hill, Shimei of the tribe of Benjamin cursed David, threw stones at him, and said, "God is now judging you because you took the throne of Saul." David's people wanted to kill Shimei, but David would not allow it. He said:

> ... so let him curse, for Jehovah has said to him, Curse David! ... let him alone and let him curse; for Jehovah has bidden him. It may be that Jehovah will look on mine affliction, and that Jehovah will requite me good for my being cursed this day (II Samuel 16:10-12).

David fled from Jerusalem over the River Jordan into the Trans-Jordan area. Out of the distress of his heart, he wrote these words:

As the hart panteth after the water-brooks, so panteth my soul after thee, O God.

The hart, or stag, or male deer, is a beautiful animal—swift in action, very sensitive, watchful, alert; but the one great desire of these animals is water. He pants for the water-brooks. We are told that a hart seeks after water not only to satisfy its thirst, but when it is pursued by a hunter, it tries to find the brooks in order to cover his scent.

If you notice a hart at the water-brook, you can see how it longs after it, and it literally pants. So David said:

> As the hart panteth after the water-brooks, so panteth my soul after thee, O God.

Dear brothers and sisters, think of the situation. David was dethroned by his son, and he was in exile. When a person is in exile, he will probably be planning on how to regain his kingdom, planning his revenge. No doubt he would be thinking of what he had lost—the kingdom, the throne—but with David, it was different. Even though plans were laid as to how to fight against the rebellion and regain the throne and the kingdom, yet in the very heart of David, it was not the kingdom, the throne, the people, the glory, the honor, the wealth, or the land. No. The thing that was deepest in his heart was God. He did not mind too much about the loss of a kingdom, but there was one thing which he panted after, and that was God. He was willing to lose everything except God.

My soul thirsteth for God, for the living God:
when shall I come and appear before God?

Oh, how his soul panted after God! Like a hart, he was thirsty for God. He was heaving within his soul for God. "O God, where are You? When shall I appear before You?" This was the one longing of his heart! Is this not the normal condition of a child of God? Of course, when one is in a time of trouble, he may certainly be panting after God; but in ordinary days when everything is peaceful and calm, should we not pant after God as a hart panteth after the water-brooks? He is life to us! He is water to us! We are told that people can live without food for days, but they cannot live without water for long. Thirstiness is even more painful than hunger. Should we not hunger and thirst after righteousness—after God? Should not that be our one passion—God himself? There is a famous saying by Saint Augustine in his confession: "God, my soul is made for Thee. I could never find rest for my soul until I rest in Thee."

Are we restless? Are we panting? Is there an upheaval within our soul? Why then are we restless? Is it because of some material thing, some earthly loss, or is it because of God? Do we ever pant after God and have that feeling that we are thirsty unto death? The Scripture says in Matthew 5:

> Blessed they who hunger and thirst after righteousness, for they shall be filled (v.6).

If that is true, we shall be filled with God. The reason we have so little of Him is that we are not hungry and thirsty after Him. We feel comfortable even if we do not have the sense of His presence. Though we do not have the sweet communion with Him, we still think we can live.

But oh, if you are a hart, you will not live without water! If you are a soul that is like David, you will not be able to live without God—not for a moment.

My soul thirsteth for God,
for the living God

God is the God of life. This is not an insignificant matter. It is a life or death matter—whether you have communion with God or are deprived of that fellowship with Him. David knew this, and he thirsted for the living God.

when shall I come
and appear before God?

This is almost like a paradox. When the priests carrying the ark came to David, in typology, it meant God was going with David into exile. But David told the priests to go back to the city. He did not want to see the ark of God wander again. It had wandered through the wilderness for forty years and in the land for hundreds of years until it was moved by David to Mount Zion in the tent of David. It was his desire that the ark of God should come to rest. Yet when David was in Mahanaim on the eastern side of Jordan, how he longed and said, "When shall I come and appear before God?"

In one sense, God is omnipresent—whether it is Jerusalem or Mahanaim, God is certainly there with David. On the other hand, as you read in the Old Testament, God told Moses that after the children of Israel entered into the promised land, He would choose a place to put His Name. The twelve tribes must go there to offer sacrifices and worship. They were not allowed to do this anywhere in the promised land. They had to go to Jerusalem to the place of God's choice. So it was true that God was with David and had never left him; yet, he was away from the place where God's Name was—Jerusalem. He was away from the tent and the congregation that gathered before God to worship. Because of this, he felt the loss of it.

Applying this to us today, we realize that wherever we are and in whatever circumstances we may be, God has never left us nor forsaken us. In the Gospel of John, the Lord Jesus said,

> ... and he will give you another Comforter, that he may be with you for ever, ... for he abides with you, and shall be in you (14:16-17).

In the New Testament time, we are in a better position than those Old Testament saints. In that time, God was with them but not in them. Therefore, it is true now that God is present at all times. However, there are times when we lose this consciousness, and when we do, we lose our very life. Our strength is gone; our faith is gone; our joy is gone; our hope is gone! When we enter into such darkness, oh how our soul cries out "… for the living God … when shall I come and appear before God?"

It is true that we do not worship in Jerusalem nor on Mount Gerizim. We worship in spirit and truth. God is Spirit and is seeking for true worshippers. It is no longer a concern of time or place (see John 4:20-24). God does say, "For where two or three are gathered together unto my name, there am I in the midst of them" (Matthew 18:20). And we are exhorted to not forsake the gathering together of the saints (see Hebrews 10:25). God is in us and with us; but, there is a difference. When we are gathered together with the saints, there is an extra presence of God that we do not find when alone. This is something that David missed. And we, too, will miss this if we keep ourselves from it.

"When shall I come and appear before God?" There is another translation which is a more literal one, "When do I enter and see the face of God?" (Youngs) There is nothing more vital in our Christian life than the face of God. What is the face of God?

When Moses interceded for the children of Israel, God answered him with grace and mercy. Moses dared to ask, "Let me, I pray thee, see thy glory" (Exodus 33:18). God answered him, "Thou canst not see my face … thou shalt see me from behind; but my face shall not be seen" (Exodus 33:20, 23). So God hid Moses in the cleft of the rock, and when the glory of God passed by, Moses saw the back of God. How precious must be the face of God! Do you know that we today are privileged to see the face of God?

Notice these verses in II Corinthians:

> Because it is the God who spoke that out of darkness light should shine who has shone in our hearts for the shining forth of the knowledge of the glory of God in the face of Jesus Christ (4:6).

> Now the Lord is the Spirit, but where the Spirit of the Lord is, there is liberty. But we all, looking on the glory of the Lord, with unveiled face, are transformed according to the same image from glory to glory, even as by the Lord the Spirit (3:17-18).

We see "God in the face of Jesus Christ." We can look into the glory of the Lord "with unveiled face." The veil is rent! Now we can be face to face with God. Dear brothers and sisters, this is the highest privilege that has been granted to us in mercy and grace.

What is the face of God? First of all, it is the full revelation of God. If you see His face, you see Him in all His fullness. If you see His back, you see some of His features, but you don't see Him as He is. Why are we privileged to see Him as He is? Because the Church is

> his body, the fullness of him who fills all and in all (Ephesians 1:23).

We need so much to see His face since the more we see Him, the more we know Him. One day we shall see Him as He is, and we shall be like Him (see I John 3:2), but you do not have to wait until that day. It has already begun. We see His face daily, for we are not veiled. If our heart is turned towards Him, we shall see His face. He will reveal himself to us, and we shall know Him.

Also, out of this seeing of Him, we shall be like Him. Now seeing His face is not just seeing; it is to be in His immediate presence. When we are there, He will begin to communicate himself to us, and we will be "transformed from glory to glory according to his image." This is so important to our daily living.

Dear brothers and sisters, do you long to see Him? Do you "pant" to see His face? What if He hides himself from you? If this happens to you, do you not feel as though you are dead? It is then you cry out, "Let me see Thy face!" May I share with you something of my own secret? Sometimes in my prayer before God, when it seems I am losing sight of His face, I ask: "Even if I can't see Your smiling face, let me see Your angry face. I want to see Your face." There is nothing more important than this, and it is our great need. This was the cry of David:

when shall I come and appear before God? My
tears have been my bread day and night, while
they say unto me all the day,
Where is Thy God?

David's greatest trouble was not his son Absalom and the people who rebelled against him; it was that he seemed to lose the consciousness of God's presence—*that* he could not bear. Tears became his bread day and night. Dear brothers and sisters, do we shed tears? But for what purpose? Oftentimes it is because we pity ourselves. We love ourselves so much. When we do not get what we think we should, we weep. But have we ever shed tears for God, weeping because we want Him?

> Tears have been my bread day and night and the enemy comes in and says, Where is your God?

Oh, the need of the consciousness of His abiding presence! Nothing else in your life really matters. If God is with you, who can be against you? There is nothing to be afraid of. But when you lose the consciousness of His presence, you really are in the valley of the shadow of death. This troubled David more than anything else.

These things I have remembered and have poured out my soul within me: how I passed along with the multitude, how I went on with them to the house of God, with the voice of joy and praise, a festive multitude.

When you are in trouble, and it seems like God has left you, probably one thing that will deepen your distress is the recalling of the happy times in the past. This seems to add anguish to you. But on the other hand, remembering what God has done for you does lift you out of your pit. This is a paradox. In one way, it deepens your sorrow, and in another, it brings you back to God.

Why art thou cast down, my soul, and art disquieted in me? hope in God; for I shall yet praise him, for the health of his countenance.

The spirit in David was talking to his soul. Faith was talking to fear, "Why art thou cast down, my soul?" A literal translation is: "Why do you cast yourself down, my soul?" We think it is our circumstances that cast us down, or maybe it is people or even the trouble, but no, we cast ourselves down. Brothers and sisters, remember this:
When you look at *your circumstances*, you are down.
When you look at *people*, you are down.
When you look at *the problem*, you are down.
When you look *within yourself*, you are down.
You are not supposed to look at all these. What you should do is look

> steadfastly on Jesus the leader and completer of faith (Hebrews 12:2).

When you do this, you are brought up. Your spirit will say to your soul,

hope in God

There is hope in God. In you, there is no hope. That is true. In the circumstances, there is no hope. That is always true. In people, you have no hope nor help; but God is the God of hope. You see, when the spirit begins to talk to the soul, the spirit will lift the soul out of depression.

... hope in God; for I shall yet praise Him.

That is faith! David hoped in God, so he had the faith that he would yet praise Him. God would get him out of all of these troubles.

... for the health of his countenance.

The word translated as *health* is also translated as *salvation*. The word translated as *countenance* is the same as *face*. This may be translated as, "for the salvation of his face." In other words, David knew he would yet see the face of God. His spirit began to rise up—"hope in God." It was then that the salvation of the face of God came upon him. He saw God again. The clouds were lifted, and he saw the face of God. How healthy was the face of God!

So here you will find the sons of Korah in full sympathy with David because they too had gone through deep waters which only increased their longing for God. If anyone longs for God, he will not be disappointed. He shall see the salvation of the face of God. May God help us!

2—Psalm 44: Faith

Psalm 44—To the chief Musician.
Of the sons of Korah. An instruction.

O God, with our ears have we heard, our fathers have told us, the work thou wroughtest in their days, in the days of old:

Thou, by thy hand, didst dispossess the nations, but them thou didst plant; thou didst afflict the peoples, but them didst thou cause to spread out.

For not by their own sword did they take possession of the land, neither did their own arm save them; but thy right hand, and thine arm, and the light of thy countenance, because thou hadst delight in them.

Thou thyself art my king, O God: command deliverance for Jacob.

Through thee will we push down our adversaries; through thy name will we tread them under that rise up against us.

For I will not put confidence in my bow, neither shall my sword save me.

For thou hast saved us from our adversaries, and hast put them to shame that hate us.

In God will we boast all the day, and we will praise thy name for ever. Selah.

But thou hast cast off, and put us to confusion, and dost not go forth with our armies;

Thou hast made us to turn back from the adversary, and they that hate us spoil for themselves;

Thou hast given us over like sheep appointed for meat, and hast scattered us among the nations;

Thou hast sold thy people for nought, and hast not increased thy wealth by their price;

Thou makest us a reproach to our neighbours, a mockery and a derision for them that are round about us;

Thou makest us a byword among the nations, a shaking of the head among the peoples.

All the day my confusion is before me, and the shame of my face hath covered me,

Because of the voice of him that reproacheth and blasphemeth; by reason of the enemy and the avenger.

All this is come upon us; yet have we not forgotten thee, neither have we dealt falsely against thy covenant:

Our heart is not turned back, neither have our steps declined from thy path;

Though thou hast crushed us in the place of jackals, and covered us with the shadow of death.

If we had forgotten the name of our God, and stretched out our hands to a strange *god,

Would not God search this out? for he knoweth the secrets of the heart.

But for thy sake are we killed all the day long; we are reckoned as sheep for slaughter.

Awake, why sleepest thou, Lord? arise, cast us not off for ever.

Wherefore hidest thou thy face, and forgettest our affliction and our oppression?

For our soul is bowed down to the dust; our belly cleaveth unto the earth.

Rise up for our help, and redeem us for thy loving-kindness' sake.

Of the sons of Korah.

Psalm 44 is another of the Psalms of the sons of Korah. We mentioned before that the sons of Korah were spared from destruction through the mercy of God, and because they had gone through the experience of the cross, they appreciated God in a special way. They were called to be singers in the temple.

An instruction

This Psalm is called an instruction. In other words, there is a lesson to be taught. In Psalm 42 and 43, there is the lesson of hope; in Psalm 44, the lesson of faith; and in Psalm 45, the lesson of love.

> And now abide faith, hope, love; these three things (I Corinthians 13:13).

These are the three essentials of our Christian life and are things we need to learn very much before God.

Faith to the Psalmist and the sons of Korah is not a theory or theology but a living reality. It was something they had experienced in their life; in fact, it was a way of life to them. And is it not true that faith is the way of our life? Faith is the gift of God, not something we can manufacture or work up. Oftentimes people try to work up faith, and it is fake.

> For ye are saved by grace, through faith; and this not of yourselves; it is God's gift: not on the principle of works, that no one might boast (Ephesians 2:8-9).

Even though faith is the gift of God, it is also something we need to learn as we walk before God. No one is born with faith. In Romans 10:17 we are told,

> So faith then is by report, but the report by God's word.

When the word of God is reported, it needs to be received, and when that happens, faith comes forth. The father of faith, Abraham, was not born with faith. It was through his obedience, trials, and even his failures that he learned faith. Any gift of God needs to be received. Then it becomes our portion.

In modern history, there is one who is known as a man of faith—George Mueller. He was a German, and he went to England to study to be a missionary to the Jews. But while he was doing that, the Lord changed his course. Eventually, he resided in England, and God used him to open up an orphanage. Mueller felt that Christians did not know what faith was; therefore, he founded that orphanage, and in caring for it, he never told people about his needs. He only told God. By faith, he did this marvelous work in the orphanage. In his lifetime, he had half a million prayers answered that could be traced. He was a man of faith. People would say to him, "Mueller, you must have the gift of faith." He said, "No, I don't have the gift of faith; I have the grace of faith." He received what God had given.

In this Psalm, there is the teaching on faith. We will not find faith in ourselves, nor will we find it by looking around; but, if we look to the Originator, the Giver of our faith, then we will have faith. This is what we read in Hebrews 12:2 “looking stedfastly on Jesus the leader and completer of faith.”

Outline

We may roughly divide this Psalm into four stanzas:

The Testimony of Faith (vv. 1-8)
The Testing Of Faith (vv. 9-16)
The Travail of Faith (vv. 17-22)
The Triumph of Faith (vv. 23-26)

Stanza 1: The Testimony of Faith (vv. 1-8)

How does faith arise in the heart of a person? Here the Psalmist begins with,

O God ...

Remember, these Psalms have continuity. If you read the two preceding ones, you see the Psalmist looking unto himself, and while he was doing that, his soul was cast down. He was disquieted because he was looking at his environment. He sank just like Peter when he was walking on water.

Thank God, at the beginning of Psalm 44, he said, "O God." He has now turned his eyes away from himself and his environment and has looked to God. It was then that he started to hear in a better way.

If you want to hear somebody when they are speaking, it is much better if you can look them in the face. This is also true with the hearing of God's voice. If your eyes are not upon Him, He may speak, but you don't hear, or you may not hear Him rightly. Faith begins with your eyes upon the Lord

O God, with our ears have we heard ...

Here the eyes of the Psalmist are upon the Lord, and his ears begin to hear. He heard the voice of divine history. Faith comes by report, so he heard the report. What does he hear?

... our fathers have told us, the work thou wroughtest in their days, in the days of old: Thou, by thy hand, didst dispossess the nations, but them thou didst plant; thou didst afflict the peoples, but them didst thou cause to spread out.

When his eyes are turned upon the Lord, then his ears begin to hear what God has done with the nation of Israel. God brought them out of Egypt through the terrible wilderness and into the promised land. There He dispossessed the nations and planted His people in the land. Now, this is something tremendous—how God did such a marvelous thing. The Psalmist heard the report, and his faith began to rise within him, saying that since God has done such a marvelous work unto our fathers, what is it that he cannot do for us? This is the way faith begins to rise within our hearts.

Dear brothers and sisters, have you heard what God has done for us in the past? He has not only delivered us out of the power of darkness; He has translated us into the kingdom of the Son of His love. Do you know that God has dispossessed our enemies and planted us in the promised land? We are not squatters there but planted by God in Christ Jesus. Christ is our promised land, and we are to enjoy all the riches that are in Christ. This is what God has done for us. This is divine history, and we need to hear it! If we are able to hear it afresh in the spirit, how can faith not rise up within us? It would be impossible! It is supernaturally natural for us to believe in God. Not to believe would be unnatural. Whatever we are involved in amounts to so little when we compare them with what God has already done. He has done great things!

For not by their own sword did they take possession of the land, neither did their own arm save them; but thy right hand, and thine arm, and the light of thy countenance ...

This great feat was not done by the children of Israel. They were few in number and weak, so they could not dispossess their enemies by their own sword or with their arm. No! It was very clear that it was the right hand, the arm of God, and the light of His countenance. Why did God do such a great work?

... because thou hadst delight in them.

It is according to His good pleasure—the good pleasure of His will—that he has brought us into Christ and has planted us in Him.

It is true that "faith comes by report and report by the word of God," but faith is something more. When you believe, it means that you make a commitment. If you believe, you surrender yourself to God and give yourself to obey Him.

Thou thyself art my king, O God:
command deliverance for Jacob.

As faith rose in the heart of the Psalmist, he said: "Yes, I have heard of what you have done in the past, and I believe it. I believe you are the same yesterday, today, and forever; therefore, I commit myself to you. I take you as my king. You shall have full authority over my life. I am committed to you and yield myself to you. I am going to obey you, for you are my king."

The problem with some people today is, after hearing what the Lord has done in the past and believing in God, there is no committal. Now, if you do not commit yourself to God, how can you expect Him to commit himself to you? Faith demands committal. Faith demands surrender. Faith demands obedience.

We have to take Him as our King, and if we do, then our King shall rule over us and over all things for us. It is then—on the basis of that committal and obedience—that we can ask God to "command deliverance for Jacob."

Through thee will we push down our adversaries; through thy name will we tread them under that rise up against us.
For I will not put confidence in my bow, neither shall my sword save me.

Here he takes a position of faith. He believes in God and believes that He will save him. He will not put confidence in himself. This position of faith is one which we must take, and when we do, we will declare, "For thou hast saved us from our adversaries, and hast put them to shame that hate us."

Notice the tense here. When he takes the position of faith and declares it, it becomes something that God has already done, "Thou hast…Thou hast." Of course, we know when the Psalmist declares this as a testimony, he wasn't really delivered—but he was delivered. The experience of deliverance had not yet happened, but the faith of it had. This is what we read of in Mark 11:24:

> All things whatsoever ye pray for and ask, believe that ye receive it, and it shall come to pass for you.

In other words, if you have faith, real faith in God, then by faith, you have already received what is coming to pass. First, you receive it by faith; then you can receive it by fact.

The problem with us is that we want to receive it by fact before we receive it by faith. In this case, it is not faith; it is sight. Faith is something that has not come to pass in fact yet, but, in faith, it has already been done. If you believe you have received it, then you shall receive it.

I remember what dear brother Nee said about faith. "Faith is not only believing that God is able; of course, He is able; He is omnipotent. Faith is not only believing God is willing; of course, God is willing; He is love. Faith is believing God has done it."

Now you say, how can this be? This is the same as Hebrews 11:1: "Now faith is the substantiating of things hoped for ..." Faith makes real the unseen. It is still unseen, yet faith has believed it; therefore, faith substantiates it before the substance is realized. Because of that, the Psalmist says,

In God will we boast all the day, and we will
praise thy name for ever.

He begins to praise. Now you cannot praise if you are still in the stage of begging. You start to praise when, by faith, you have apprehended what God has promised. This is what's called the testimony of faith. Usually, when you give a testimony, you would have to experience it first; but, the testimony of faith is different. You testify before it comes because you know it is coming. It is the testimony of faith.

Selah

Notice the word *Selah* at the end of verse 8. In Hebrew, *selah* means a pause or a rest. It is just like in music where you come to a place that calls for a rest. Also, *selah* is not only a pause for meditation in quietness; but it is a time when you may gather up more strength to go on to that which is to follow. In other words, you will rise to a higher note; so, you need to pause and breathe to prepare yourself to sing a higher note.

Do we know *selah* in our lives? Sometimes in our individual lives, we need to pause. We cannot go on being excited all the time because very soon, we will be exhausted. Then there will be a reaction. When God begins to work in our lives, we come to a point where we need to rest so that we may gather up more strength to strike a higher note. We need that *selah*.

Sometimes in our time of worship I feel we need a little *selah*. Not a long pause of death, but a *selah* of life. When the Lord is beginning to show himself to us, and we are being stirred, and our hearts are touched, then it is time that we get quiet before the Lord so we might gather up more strength to strike a higher note. If we continue being stirred, we will drop, and often this happens. We need some *selah* in the spirit. Do not think that we have to go on and on and on, just like horses that cannot stop. No! We need *selah* because something higher is to follow.

Stanza 2: The Testing of Faith (vv. 9-16)

The second stanza, begins with the word "but." Here the Psalmist seems to be full of faith, and because of that, he expects immediate deliverance. What else can he expect because he has already received it in faith, and he is waiting to receive it in fact. But the expected does not come; on the contrary, the unexpected arrives.

But thou hast cast off,
and put us to confusion,
and dost not go forth with our armies;
Thou hast made us to
turn back from the adversary,
and they that hate us spoil for themselves;
Thou hast given us over
like sheep appointed for meat,
and hast scattered us among the nations;

The Psalmist fully expected deliverance from God, from the enemy, and from oppression. He expected to be delivered into that broad place which God had promised; delivered into the riches of Christ; but, instead, the situation became worse. This is the testing of faith.

Dear brothers and sisters, do not think that faith is so simple. Do not think that just because we believe, the minute we believe, that split second, the thing happens according to what we have believed.

Sometimes it does because God knows our frailty, but often it does not. Why? Because He wants to test our faith and draw out of us the faith which He has planted within.

Remember the word in I Peter 1:6-7:

> Wherein ye exult, for a little while at present, if needed, put to grief by various trials, that the proving of your faith, much more precious than of gold which perishes, though it be proved by fire, be found to praise and glory and honour in the revelation of Jesus Christ.

Because you have faith, therefore God puts you into the fiery furnace to prove that faith so that it will be more precious than gold though it be proved by fire. This faith will be found to praise and glory and honor at the revelation of Jesus Christ. This is the testing of faith.

Sometimes we have in us a sense of heroism. And this is natural. We want to be spiritual heroes, and we try to work up faith. Oh, we have great faith in God, and because we do, God has to do it right away. But if He does, who gets the glory? We do! There is no heroism in the spiritual realm.

Remember the three friends of Daniel. King Nebuchadnezzar built a fire seven times hotter in that furnace, and these three testified to the King saying:

> If it be so, our God whom we serve is able to deliver us from the burning fiery furnace, and he will deliver us out of thy hand, O king. But if not, be it known unto thee, O king, that we will not serve thy gods, nor worship the golden image that thou hast set up (Daniel 3:17-18).

This is the testing of faith! Yes, when you believe in God, and you begin to testify of your faith, you will be put into the fiery furnace that your faith may be tried, tested, and proved until it comes out more precious than gold.

Thou hast sold thy people for nought, and hast not increased thy wealth by their price.

Oh, how often it seems that God has sold us into the hands of the enemy, and we wonder if He has made some increase by our price. Do you not sometimes feel that way when your faith is tested? If God could increase His wealth, then maybe it is worthwhile; but, it does not seem to be so. On the contrary, God's name is being put to shame. Why should God allow such things to happen? It is the trial, the testing of our faith.

Stanza 3: The Travail of Faith (vv. 17-22)

All this is come upon us; yet have we not forgotten thee, neither have we dealt falsely against thy covenant: Our heart is not turned back, neither have our steps declined from thy path.

In the testing of faith, many are crushed because their faith seems to fail and not produce the expected, anticipated results. They turn against God, saying, "God is not to be trusted. He is not there. He does not care." Brothers and sisters, when faith is tested, this is the time for the travail of faith. You have to travail in testing.

Yes, it is a death—death like a woman in travail giving birth and going through the process of death in order that life may come forth. But often we are not willing to pay the cost of travail. When things begin to get hard, we lash out at God, turn our back, and get a spiritual abortion.

But listen to the Psalmist as he is in the travail of faith. He said, "Lord, in spite of the fact that it seems as if things have gotten worse, yet we have not turned against Thee. We are still keeping our faith in Thee and we are still loyal to Thee."

Though thou hast crushed us in the place of jackals, and covered us with the shadow of death. If we had forgotten the name of our God, and stretched out our hands to a strange god, Would not God search this out? for he knoweth the secrets of the heart.

This is the travail of faith. The next verse is quoted in Romans 8:36.

But for thy sake are we killed all the day long;
we are reckoned as sheep for slaughter.

In the preceding verses, Paul gives a great testimony saying:

> What shall we then say to these things? If God be for us, who against us? He who, yea, has not spared his own Son, but delivered him up for us all, how shall he not also with him grant us all things? Who shall bring an accusation against God's elect? It is God who justifies: who is he that condemns? It is Christ who has died, but rather has been also raised up; who is also at the right hand of God; who also intercedes for us. (Romans 8:31-34)

After this great testimony, notice what follows:

> Who shall separate us from the love of Christ? tribulation or distress, or persecution, or famine, or nakedness, or danger, or sword? (v.35)

You see, after this great declaration, faith is being tried. Satan is out trying to separate us from the love of Christ with tribulation, with distress, with persecution, with famine, with nakedness, with danger, and with sword. We are killed for the Lord's sake all day long and reckoned as sheep for slaughter. Why? Because we believe in God: "But for thy sake …" This is the travail of faith.

But that travail is not in vain. Immediately you will find these words:

> But in all these things we more than conquer through him that has loved us. For I am persuaded that neither death, nor life, nor angels, nor principalities, nor things present, nor things to come, nor powers, nor height, nor depth, nor any other creature, shall be able to separate us from the love of God, which is in Christ Jesus our Lord. (Romans 8:37-39)

Through the travail of faith, there will come forth the "more than conquer[ors] through him that has loved us."

Stanza 4: The Triumph of Faith (vv. 23-26)

Awake, why sleepest thou, Lord?
arise, cast us not off for ever.
Wherefore hidest thou thy face, and forgettest
our affliction and our oppression?
For our soul is bowed down to the dust;
our belly cleaveth unto the earth.
Rise up for our help, and redeem us
for thy loving-kindness' sake.

Since the Psalmist believed in God despite everything that had happened, and because he travailed in faith, now out comes the prayer of faith. He can pray with boldness, "Arise, awake, O God, and deliver us." And from where does this boldness to approach the throne of grace come? It comes through faithfulness. It is not because you have faith, nor is it what you are or how you believe. It is because of the loving-kindness and tender mercies of God that He answers your prayer.

In this Psalm, we are taught the great lesson of faith. Psalm 44 is a great Psalm of faith just like Hebrews 11 is a great chapter on faith. It is an instruction. May we all learn this great lesson of faith!

3—Psalm 45: Love

Psalm 45—To the chief Musician. Upon Shoshannim. Of the sons of Korah. An instruction; a song of the Beloved.

My heart is welling forth *with* a good matter: I say what I have composed touching the king. My tongue is the pen of a ready writer.

Thou art fairer than the sons of men; grace is poured into thy lips: therefore God hath blessed thee for ever.

Gird thy sword upon *thy* thigh, O mighty one, *in* thy majesty and thy splendour;

And *in* thy splendour ride prosperously, because of truth and meekness *and* righteousness: and thy right hand shall teach thee terrible things.

Thine arrows are sharp—peoples fall under thee—in the heart of the king's enemies.

Thy throne, O God, is for ever and ever; a sceptre of uprightness is the sceptre of thy kingdom:

Thou hast loved righteousness, and hated wickedness; therefore God, thy God, hath anointed thee with the oil of gladness above thy companions.

Myrrh and aloes, cassia, are all thy garments; out of ivory palaces stringed instruments have made thee glad.

Kings' daughters are among thine honourable women; upon thy right hand doth stand the queen in gold of Ophir.

Hearken, daughter, and see, and incline thine ear; and forget thine own people and thy father's house:

And the king will desire thy beauty; for he is thy Lord, and worship thou him.

And the daughter of Tyre with a gift, the rich ones among the people, shall court thy favour.

All glorious is the king's daughter within; her clothing is of wrought gold:

She shall be brought unto the king in raiment of embroidery; the virgins behind her, her companions, shall be brought in unto thee:

With joy and gladness shall they be brought; they shall enter into the king's palace.

Instead of thy fathers shall be thy sons; princes shalt thou make them in all the earth.

I will make thy name to be remembered throughout all generations; therefore shall the peoples praise thee for ever and ever.

The Psalms of the sons of Korah are very special Psalms sung by very special people. As you recall, the sons of Korah were those who were spared from destruction by the mercy of God. Since they received such mercy, out of the abundance of their heart, they sing these songs to God.

Psalms 42 and 43 spoke of our hope in God, while Psalm 44 was found to be one on faith. Now we will look at Psalm 45, which is one on love. The apostle Paul said in I Corinthians 13:13: "And now abide faith, hope, love; these three things; and the greater of these is love." Psalm 45 is a song of love.

We do not actually know who was instrumental in writing this Psalm; but, we know one thing: this Psalm is not just a romantic one. Some people think this is a song celebrating the marriage of King Solomon with one of the foreign princesses; but, we believe it is more than that. It is inspired by the Spirit of God, and it is put in the sacred pages. Why? Because it speaks of the love and the marriage of Christ and His Church.

The Song of Songs speaks of the love and the marriage union of Christ and an individual believer. In other words, it is revealing the individual believer's personal relationship to Christ and Christ's relationship to the individual believer.

However, Psalm 45 speaks of a corporate relationship. It is the love, the union, and the marriage of Christ with His Church. It is called *the song of the beloved*. In the original, it means *song of loves*. Notice "love" is in the plural form. This is because it is the love of the king towards the queen and also the love of the queen towards the king. It is love that is mutual. It is responsive love. How the king loves the queen! And how the queen loves the king!

To the chief Musician.

After this Psalm was written, it was put to music to be sung in the temple when God's people came to worship. This is not an ordinary song. It is something to be sung in the house of God as an expression of worship.

Upon Shoshannim.

This means "Upon lilies." We do not know whether this means a musical tune or a musical instrument; but, we know what lilies represent. Our Lord said,

> Observe with attention the lilies of the field, how they grow: they toil not, neither do they spin; but I say unto you, that not even Solomon in all his glory was clothed as one of these (Matthew 6:28-29).

Lilies in the Scripture speak of the heavenly care of our Father towards the lowest, the smallest, the nothing. Yet His care is so much that He can clothe the lilies with such beauty that even Solomon in all his glory cannot be compared with them. And of course, lilies speak of purity—how pure under the care of the Heavenly Father; how beautiful it can be.

An instruction.

This Psalm is also an instruction. In other words, it is a lesson for us to learn.

Now we come to one of the sweetest Psalms in the Bible—a Psalm of love. This Psalm can be divided into three parts:

Part 1—Introduction (v.1)
Part 2—The King (vv. 2-9)
Part 3—The Queen (vv. 10-17)

Part 1—Introduction (v. 1)

My heart is welling forth with a good matter: I
say what I have composed touching the king.
My tongue is the pen of a ready writer.

What is this good matter about which the Psalmist speaks? Is there any matter better than the love of Christ and His Church?

As a matter of fact, this is the whole revelation of the entire Bible. If you are able to see this, then the Bible is an open book to you. All the revelation you find in the Bible is centered upon the union of Christ and the Church. This is the great theme that goes through the entire word from Genesis to Revelation. I believe it was brother Watchman Nee who said that if you receive the revelation of Christ and the Church, then you receive the whole revelation of the Bible. It is true. You may glean a little here and there and get some moral teaching and some instruction; but, if you do not see this, then the Bible is closed to you. However, once you do see, there is no end to what is in the Bible.

Therefore you find the heart of the Psalmist is so filled with a good matter and just bubbling forth with the love and union of Christ and the Church that he cannot help but find that his tongue is like the pen of a ready writer. In other words, "out of the abundance of the heart, the mouth speaks." This is not something mechanical.

I remember when I was in college, we were required to write poems. I recall how I labored and tried to make it rhyme, but it was so mechanical. It did not come from the abundance of my heart. The Psalmist did not need to labor because his heart was so occupied with this good matter. When it says, "I say what I have composed…", in the original, *composed* means *my occupation*. He is so occupied with this good theme that his tongue is a pen of a ready writer, and it just flows and comes out as overflowing. This is how he feels about the king and the queen.

Dear brothers and sisters, is this not the way we should feel about Christ and His Church? Can we speak of Christ without any feeling within us? Can we speak of the Church without our hearts overflowing with the love of God? Can we think of the union of Christ and His Church without being deeply touched and moved in our spirit? Oh, this is not something we can talk about without any feeling, just being mechanical. This good matter should occupy our whole being all the time and should come forth naturally and spontaneously with deep feeling and love. Our tongue should be as the pen of a ready writer.

Part 2—The King (vv. 2-9)

> Thy throne, O God, is for ever and ever; a sceptre of uprightness is the sceptre of thy kingdom (Psalm 45:6).

The second part is verses 2 through 9, which touches the king. First of all, we must mention that the king is Christ.

His Life

> Thou art fairer than the sons of men; grace is poured into thy lips: therefore God hath blessed thee for ever (Psalm 45:2).

In verse 2, this speaks of our Lord Jesus's life on earth, and it does seem the Psalmist begins quite abruptly. He says,

Thou art fairer than the sons of men ...

Out of the fullness of his heart, he thinks of Christ as the son of man. God came to be a man, but he says, "Thou art fairer than the sons of men ..." He says, "You are different; You are unique; You are special!"

I remember this story about Samuel Rutherford, who was a great man of God. You might remember the hymn *Immanuel's Land* which was inspired by his life and letters. Because of his faith, he was suffering a great deal, and finally was summoned by the king to be judged. He was on his death bed at that time and responded, "I must answer my first summons; and before your day arrives, I will be where few kings and great folks come"—in Immanuel's Land.

> The sands of time are sinking,
>   the dawn of heaven breaks,
> the summer morn I've sighed for,
>   the fair sweet morn awakes;
> dark, dark hath been the midnight,
>   but dayspring is at hand,
> and glory, glory dwelleth
>   in Emmanuel's land.

In one of his letters he also wrote:

> ... and what fairer thing than Christ? O fair sun, and fair moon, and fair stars, and fair flowers, and

> fair roses, and fair lilies, and fair creatures: but O ten thousand thousand times fairer Lord Jesus! Alas, I wronged Him in making the comparison this way. O black sun and moon; but O fair Lord Jesus! O black flowers, and black lilies and roses; but O fair, fair, even fair Lord Jesus! O all fair things, black and deformed without beauty, when ye are beside that fairest Lord Jesus! O black heaven, but O fair Christ! O black angels, but O surprisingly fair Lord Jesus! I would seek no more to make me happy for evermore but a thorough and clear sight of the beauty of Jesus my Lord. Let my eyes enjoy His fairness, and look Him for ever in the face, and I have all that can be wished.

Dear brothers and sisters, our Lord Jesus is so fair He cannot be compared with anyone or anything. When we try to compare, it means it is still comparable, but our Lord Jesus is so different. He is the only One who is sinless-perfect. There is no comparison.

As the Psalmist sings of the fairness of the Lord Jesus, he thinks especially of one thing, which is,

grace is poured into thy lips.

The apostle John said,

> And the Word became flesh, and dwelt among us (and we have contemplated his glory, a glory as of

an only-begotten with a father), full of grace and truth (John 1:14).

You know, we are sons of men, and as such, we demand and require of others. But, our Lord Jesus is fairer. Instead of demanding and requiring—and He surely has every right and is qualified to do this—He gives. This is grace! Grace is undeserved favor, and this is what our Lord Jesus gives all the time.

Remember the woman caught in adultery who was led by the Jewish people to the Lord Jesus and accused before the crowd? They said, "Teacher, this woman has been taken in the very act, committing adultery. Now in the law Moses has commanded us to stone such; thou therefore, what sayest thou?" (John 8:4-5). Oh, how the people demanded for that woman; but, what was probably on their minds was not death for the woman but death for Christ Jesus. If He would say, "Let her be stoned," then they would say, "Where is your love?" Also, to keep the Law of Moses would be to violate the law of Caesar because the Roman government took away from the Jews the power of sentencing people to death. If He set her free, then He would violate the Law of Moses, and those who did this deserved to die. Through this, they tried to trap Jesus. They demanded His death.

But look at His response. He stooped down and wrote with His finger on the sand. When they pressed Him, He stood up and said, "Let him that is without sin among you first cast the stone at her" (John 8:7). Then He again stooped down and wrote on the ground. There was too much shame to look at that woman. There was too much shame to look at the crowd. Then they went out one by one from the oldest to the youngest. They were convicted. Then the Lord Jesus got up and said, "Woman, where are those thine accusers? Has no one condemned thee? And she said, No one, sir. And Jesus said to her, Neither do I condemn thee: go, and sin no more" (John 8:10-11). This is grace! Brothers and sisters, haven't you heard this word from the lips of our Lord Jesus?

When we first came to the Lord Jesus loaded down with sins under the curse of the Law, and there was no hope, then we heard that word of grace from the lips of our Lord Jesus, "Your sins are forgiven you. Go in peace." Also, we oftentimes hear the word of the Lord, "Fear not, I am with you." Oh, think of the grace of our Lord Jesus and how He dispenses it to us who are so unworthy and undeserving.

Therefore, God hath blessed thee for ever.

Three times the heavens were opened, and the word was, "This is my beloved Son in whom I have found my delight." There is no wonder about that. Think of our King, our Lord Jesus, and His life on earth. How full of grace and truth He is!

His Work

> Gird thy sword upon thy thigh, O mighty one, in thy majesty and thy splendour; And in thy splendour ride prosperously, because of truth and meekness and righteousness: and thy right hand shall teach thee terrible things. Thine arrows are sharp—peoples fall under thee—in the heart of the king's enemies (Psalm 45:3-5).

In verses 3, 4, and 5, it speaks of our Lord's work. When He was on the earth and walked among men, He was such a humble person. As He walked from Jerusalem to Galilee and passed through Samaria, He did many good things. Yet, in the eyes of the world, He was accused and put to death on Calvary's cross. In the eyes of those who see, and in the eyes of the Psalmist, it is a different picture. Instead of a humble man forsaken, despised, persecuted, and crucified, they see a great warrior with his

... sword upon thy thigh, O mighty one, in thy majesty and thy splendour. And in thy splendour ride prosperously

Here He rises forth to conqueror all His enemies and the world. How does He conquer?

because of truth and meekness
and righteousness

"because of truth"—This world is full of lies, and the ruler of this world, Satan, is the greatest liar. The whole world system is under a lie. Lying is more than just telling an untruth. Sometimes people tell something which is not true; they are false, and we say it is a lie. Or sometimes we try to defend ourselves and say it is a white lie, not a black lie. But it is still a lie.

"and meekness"—Meekness is the opposite of selfishness. Meekness means "selflessness." We are self-centered and think of ourselves all the time. Everything is for self. Self-interest is at the very center of this world, and self is at the very center of each of our lives. However, our Lord Jesus came to conquer this with meekness.

> for I am meek and lowly in heart; and ye shall find rest to your souls (Matthew 11:30).

Why is there restlessness in our souls? It is because we are selfish and think only of ourselves. If we were selfless, we would have rest in our souls. Our Lord Jesus thinks only of doing the Father's will. "…not my will, but thine be done" (Luke 22:42). This is meekness, and He conquers the world with it.

"and righteousness"—Our Lord also conquers the world with righteousness. This world is full of evil and wicked things that are not right in the sight of God.

Yes, we do have self-righteousness sometimes, but in the sight of God, everything is wrong, evil, and wicked.

Our Lord Jesus comes and brings righteousness to us because we have no righteousness of our own: "… all our righteousnesses are as filthy rags" (Isaiah 64:6). God has clothed us with Christ as our righteousness (see I Corinthians 1:30) which gives us a standing before God. Since the life of Christ is within us, we can now practice righteousness in our daily life as the Apostle John said: "… every one who practises righteousness is begotten of him" (I John 2:29).

and thy right hand shall teach thee
terrible things. Thine arrows are sharp
—peoples fall under thee
—in the heart of the king's enemies.

Is it not true that when the word of God comes to us, it is as an arrow? Men's words aim at our mind, but God's words aim at the heart. You do not shoot an arrow at random. You set a target and aim for it. Here the word of our Lord comes like arrows piercing our hearts, and we are smitten and fall at His feet.

Oh, dear brothers and sisters, how we do praise and thank God that He overcomes us, convicts us, and brings us to our knees! How He conquers us with His truth, meekness, and righteousness! This speaks of the work of our Lord Jesus the King. He said, "I have been born for this. My kingdom is not of this world. I have come into the world, that I might bear witness to the truth" (John 18:37). His kingdom is a kingdom of truth, meekness, and righteousness.

His Glory

> Thy throne, O God, is for ever and ever; a sceptre of uprightness is the sceptre of thy kingdom: Thou hast loved righteousness, and hated wickedness; therefore God, thy God, hath anointed thee with the oil of gladness above thy companions (Psalm 45:6-7).

Thy throne, O God,
is for ever and ever

These two verses speak of His glory. Our Lord Jesus came into this world and was born a King, yet He lived a humble life. He did a tremendous work conquering by truth, meekness, and righteousness. After He completed His work, He ascended up on high and was given a throne, and His throne "is for ever and ever."

a sceptre of uprightness is
the sceptre of thy kingdom

This verse is quoted in Hebrews to prove that our Lord Jesus is far superior than the angels. The angels are ministering servants, but our Lord Jesus is the

Master, the Lord. His throne is an eternal throne. His scepter is a scepter of righteousness. After the Lord ascended, He received from His Father glory, honor, kingdom, and dominion. The writer of Hebrews said, "But we see Jesus, who was made some little inferior to angels on account of the suffering of death…." But notice he also says, "… crowned with glory and honour …" (2:9-11).

Thou has loved righteousness, and hated wickedness; therefore God, thy God, hath anointed thee with the oil of gladness above thy companions.

Now the pain, sufferings, and sorrows are over, and He is in heaven anointed with the oil of gladness. "He shall see of the fruit of the travail of his soul, and shall be satisfied …" (Isaiah 53:11). Oh, dear brothers and sisters, as our Lord Jesus looks down upon us—those who are the results of His travail—how His heart is gladdened, satisfied.

His Marriage

Verses 8 and 9 speak of His marriage. First, it is His life, then work, then glory, and now His marriage. Here He is ready for that marriage.

Myrrh and aloes, cassia, are all thy garments

In other words, He has put on His wedding garments, and they are full of fragrance. Myrrh and cassia are among the ingredients that make up the holy anointing oil (see Exodus 30:23-25). Nicodemus prepared an ointment, a mixture of myrrh and aloes, to anoint the body of our Lord (see John 19:39). Our Lord is clothed with myrrh, aloes, and cassia. He is so full of fragrance. It comes from within and diffuses around Him.

out of ivory palaces stringed instruments have made thee glad

He is now in His palace, and it is ivory. If you wanted to build an ivory palace, where would you get the ivory? Think of how many elephants would have to suffer death for this. Out of sufferings come forth the beautiful ivory palace. In other words, He builds His palace with His sufferings. Out of His sufferings, He has found His dwelling place.

Of course, there will be musical instruments because there will be appreciation. We, who are His ivory palaces, are the people who shall play these musical instruments to satisfy His heart.

Kings' daughters are among thine honourable women; upon thy right hand doth stand the queen in gold of Ophir.

Here you will find these honorable women individually and collectively. The queen is arrayed in the gold of Ophir, which is the finest of pure gold.

Part 3—The Queen (vv. 10-17)

The verses which we have considered so far have spoken of the king—his life, his work, his glory, and his marriage. These next ones—verses 10 through 17—speak of the queen.

> Hearken, daughter, and see, and incline thine ear; and forget thine own people and thy father's house: And the king will desire thy beauty; for he is thy Lord, and worship thou him.

An Exhortation to the Queen

Hearken, daughter ...
and forget thine own people
and thy father's house.

What is this saying? There is a call that goes out to those who are to compose that queen: "Hearken, daughter ..." They are called to forget their father's house and their own people. Are these words familiar to you?

Remember when God called Abraham: "And Jehovah had said to Abram, Go out of thy land, and from thy kindred, and from thy father's house, to the land that I will shew thee. And Abram departed as Jehovah had said to him" (Genesis 12:1, 4). Abraham went to the place of God's choice.

Ruth said these words to her mother-in-law: "… thy people shall be my people, and thy God my God" (Ruth 1:16). She was willing to leave her native land, her own people and house, in order to go with Naomi into the land of Israel.

Recall the story of Rebecca. When Abraham's steward came and claimed her to be a bride for Isaac, he rose the next morning prepared to go; but, the family said, "Let the maiden abide with us some days, or say ten; after that she shall go." The steward replied, "Do not hinder me, seeing Jehovah has prospered my way." Then it was asked of Rebecca, "Wilt thou go with this man?" And she said, "I will go." (see Genesis 24:55-56, 58).

Do you not hear the Lord Jesus say, "Come and follow Me"? And when you hear this call, how will you respond? Notice the following calls of the Lord.

> And walking by the sea of Galilee, he saw two brothers, Simon called Peter, and Andrew his brother, casting a net into the sea, for they were fishers; and he says to them, Come after me, and I will make you fishers of men. And they, having left their trawl-nets, immediately followed him. And going on thence he saw other two brothers, James the son of Zebedee and John his brother, in the ship with Zebedee their father, mending their trawl-nets, and he called them; and they,

> having left the ship and their father, immediately followed him (Matthew 4:18-22).
>
> And Jesus, passing on thence, saw a man sitting at the tax-office, called Matthew, and says to him, Follow me. And he rose up and followed him (Matthew 9:9).

Do you want to be queen to the king? Well, if you do want to be part of that queen, then the exhortation is, "Forget your own people and your father's house."

In other words, we have to abandon ourselves to the Lord. If we still hold on to the old, earthly ties or to what we consider as our own, then, dear brothers and sisters, he who does not deny himself, take up His cross, and follow the Lord is not fit to be His disciple (see Matthew 10:38). In order to be part of the queen, we must lay down everything—everything which speaks of the old relationship, the old position, the past—and be abandoned to God, abandoned to Christ. Oh, God demands that abandonment!

Think of the abandonment of the king! In order to come to us and save us, He abandoned everything. He emptied himself, taking upon himself the likeness of man, the form of a slave, and further humbled himself being obedient to the Father even unto death and that the death of the cross (see Philippians 2:6-8).

How He abandoned everything for love's sake! And love asks of you a similar abandonment. Are you abandoned to Christ, or are you still holding on to something?

Her Beauty

What is the beauty of the queen? Her beauty is her utter devotedness to the king whom she loves. Her beauty is her abandonment. And if you forget your own people and your father's house, then:

the king will desire thy beauty

Is the king desiring that you should do something for Him? Yes, it is true you must serve Him, but that is not what He desires. He desires your beauty, which is your utter abandonment to Him.

for he is thy Lord,
and worship thou him.

He has bought you with a price: His own precious blood. You are His, and you have no right to remember your own people or your father's house. You have no right to be your own, but it is right for you to abandon yourself to Him. If you know He is your Lord, then you will worship Him.

Dear brothers and sisters, how do we worship Christ? Sometimes when we come together to worship, we find ourselves unable to worship. Is worship just singing some hymns and saying some words of praise? Is this all? No. True worship is abandonment to God. Worship is a life and not something we do for an hour or something we try to do. Not at all. It is a devoted, dedicated, abandoned life to the Lord. The Lord appreciates that kind of worship more than people coming and saying just a few words. Now I do not mean that we should not say those words. We should. He wants us to express our worship. Oh, I do hope that many brothers and sisters will feel free to express thanks and appreciation to the Lord in praises and songs! The Lord appreciates all of these. But remember beyond all these—beyond time and space—there is a life that really sees Jesus as the Lord. This is the worship that He looks for. The heavenly Father is looking for true worshipers—those who worship Him in spirit and truth (see John 4:23-24). And we know who these are: the ones abandoned to the Lord.

And the daughter of Tyre with a gift,
the rich ones among the people,
shall court thy favour.

This verse is connected with verses 10 and 11. When you abandon yourself as you should, you realize that even the richest in the world—as represented by the daughter of Tyre, which is a commercial, seafaring city—can not be compared with the riches possessed by the queen. Everybody will come and ask for her favor. She can dispense the grace of God to many. This is what the Church ought to be.

The Wedding of the Queen to the King

All glorious is the king's daughter within; her clothing is of wrought gold: She shall be brought unto the king in raiment of embroidery; the virgins behind her, her companions, shall be brought in unto thee

She is ready for the wedding and is all glorious within. Remember this word in Ephesians chapter 5:

> ... even as the Christ also loved the assembly, and has delivered himself up for it, in order that he might sanctify it, purifying it by the washing of water by the word, that he might present the assembly to himself glorious, having no spot, or wrinkle, or any of such things; but that it might be holy and blameless (vv. 25-27).

So far as the king's daughter is concerned, she is all glorious within, just full of glory. What is glory? It is hard to define, but let's say that whenever God appears, you see glory. It is when God is satisfied. When this happens, the glory of the Lord will fill the temple (see II Chronicles 7:1). Here we see that the life of the king's daughter has satisfied God so much that His glory just fills her. This is what the Church is, the body of Christ, "the fullness of Him who fills all and in all."

The transformation is so complete that Christ has become all and in all to her; therefore, all glorious is the king's daughter within. There is no shade or shadow or darkness—nothing of self. It is all of Christ.

her clothing is of wrought gold

Notice the queen is dressed in two garments for the wedding. The inner garment "is of wrought gold"—a golden garment. This speaks of the best robe. When the prodigal son came back, the father put on him the best robe, which speaks of Christ our righteousness. Why is it "wrought" gold? Gold speaks of God's nature, and it is wrought or worked because Christ has come into this world and died for us. Work has been done on that gold, and yet Christ has become our righteousness. Now over and above being clothed with this garment of wrought gold—which is Christ our righteousness—there is this:

She shall be brought unto the king
in raiment of embroidery

In other words, Christ, our righteousness, who gives us standing before God, will by the Holy Spirit patiently embroider into our lives His beauty and His character. This will be like a raiment of embroidery. We see this in Revelation 19:

> Let us rejoice and exult, and give him glory; for the marriage of the Lamb is come, and his wife has made herself ready. And it was given to her that she should be clothed in fine linen, bright and pure; for the fine linen is the righteousnesses of the saints (vv. 7-8).

We have not only put on Christ as our righteousness, but the Holy Spirit will so work in our lives that the very nature of Christ will become our character. These two garments prepare us for the wedding. Thank God that all who believe in the Lord Jesus have the garment of wrought gold. But do we also have the raiment of embroidery? We are only ready for the wedding when we have put on both of these two garments.

the virgins behind her, her companions,
shall be brought in unto thee

The virgins are there as bridesmaids. In typology, the virgins represent individual believers and the queen represents the corporate church. Therefore the virgins are part of the queen, and you do not classify them into two different categories.

With joy and gladness shall they be brought;
they shall enter into the king's palace.

Remember the parable in Matthew 25 of the ten virgins. The five wise had extra oil in their vessels, and when the cry comes at midnight to come to meet the bridegroom, they will enter into the marriage feast. "With joy and gladness shall they be brought; they shall enter into the king's palace." In other words, they will enter into the glory of the millennium kingdom of the heavens.

Instead of thy fathers shall be thy sons; princes shalt thou make them in all the earth. I will make thy name to be remembered throughout all generations; therefore shall the peoples praise thee for ever and ever.

These last two verses tell of the glory during the millennium age. Out of that marriage, union comes forth: the princes who shall rule and reign with Christ for one thousand years. Speaking collectively, it is the marriage feast, and then you find those overcomers are like the princes that rule with Christ.

Next, you find the name of the Lord Jesus shall be remembered forever, and His praises shall continue forever and ever.

So, dear brothers and sisters, this is a song of loves. It tells us of the king and queen and their union. May the Lord help us to enter into the spirit of this song.

4—Psalm 46: Victory

Psalm 46—To the chief Musician.
Of the sons of Korah. On Alamoth. A song.

God is our refuge and strength, a help in distresses, very readily found.

Therefore will we not fear though the earth be removed, and though the mountains be carried into the heart of the seas;

Though the waters thereof roar and foam, though the mountains shake with the swelling thereof. Selah.

There is a river the streams whereof make glad the city of God, the sanctuary of the habitations of the Most High.

God is in the midst of her; she shall not be moved: God shall help her at the dawn of the morning.

The nations raged, the kingdoms were moved; he uttered his voice, the earth melted.

Jehovah of hosts is with us; the God of Jacob is our high fortress. Selah.

Come, behold the works of Jehovah, what desolations he hath made in the earth:

He hath made wars to cease unto the end of the earth; he breaketh the bow, and cutteth the spear in sunder; he burneth the chariots in the fire.

Be still, and know that I am God: I will be exalted among the nations, I will be exalted in the earth.

Jehovah of hosts is with us; the God of Jacob is our high fortress. Selah.

Of the sons of Korah

In considering the previous Psalms, we have mentioned who the sons of Korah were. They may also be called *the sons of the cross.* Out of their deep experience, they became singers in the house of God. They knew how to sing from the fullness of their heart. These sons of Korah were called upon to sing Psalm 46.

On Alamoth. A song.

It is sung on Alamoth, which means "virgins." Probably this was sung with high notes because it is a song of victory—a song of great rejoicing. In verse 14 of the preceding Psalm—"She shall be brought unto the king in raiment of embroidery; the virgins behind her, her companions, shall be brought in unto thee."—we have the marriage of the king and the queen which typifies the marriage union of Christ and His Church. Virgins here refer to individual believers, and the queen refers to believers collectively. So following the preceding Psalm, we now have this Psalm 46 to be sung with virgin voices who sing the victory of the Lord.

The Scripture never speaks of the people of this world as virgins. So far as spiritual sense is concerned, people in this world are considered before God as adulterers and adulteresses, defiled by this world system. Only the redeemed of the Lord are considered virgins since they are washed by the precious blood of the Lamb. They are as virgins unto God. Paul said in II Corinthians:

> For I am jealous as to you with a jealousy which is of God; for I have espoused you unto one man, to present you a chaste virgin to Christ. But I fear lest by any means, as the serpent deceived Eve by his craft, so your thoughts should be corrupted from simplicity as to the Christ (11:2-3).

We who are the redeemed of the Lord, purchased by the blood, are virgins in God's sight and should keep our virginity, our chastity, before Him. We have been espoused to Christ and are waiting for Him, for that day of the marriage union.

But before that comes, we as virgins must keep our virginity to the Lord. It is not an easy job. The enemy, the world, sin, the flesh, everything tries to corrupt us and destroy our chastity towards God. But, thank God, through it all, we find God able to keep us until the day of Christ. Through every trouble, all kinds of temptations, through the tempest and the roaring sea, God is able to keep those who are His. So may the background of this Psalm help us as we consider it together.

This is considered as Luther's Psalm. Martin Luther, the great reformer, and his companions were willing to sacrifice their lives for the work of the Lord. We might think that he and his companions certainly knew no fear and had no despair because surely they had "lion" hearts. But if we know human beings, we have to realize that their hearts would grow faint at times. When this happened, Luther would say to his companion, Melanchthon, (who was younger than he and the theologian of the reformation), "Let's sing Psalm 46." Now Luther had a special translation that was in German but has been translated into English. I will just read a portion of it to give the feeling.

A sure stronghold, our God is He,
A timely shield and weapon;
Our help He'll be and set us free
From every ill can happen.

And were the world with devils filled,
All eager to devour us,
Our souls to fear should little yield,
They cannot overpower us.

As they sang this, their spirits were lifted, and they were able to go on with God's work of reformation.

This Psalm is divided into three parts, as you can readily see because all of them end with *Selah*. As mentioned before, *Selah* means to pause or rest. It is not a passive thing, but is very active.

Part 1—The Tempest (vv. 1-3)

Part 2—The Secret (vv. 4-7)

Part 3—The Calm of Victory (vv. 8-11)

Part 1—The Tempest (vv. 1-3)

God is our refuge and strength,
a help in distresses, very readily found.

When the virgins began to sing this song, it was with a declaration of their faith, their full confidence in God: "God is our refuge." To understand this, we have to have some historical background.

God commanded Moses that after the children of Israel arrived in Canaan, they should set apart cities of refuge—three on the east side of Jordan and three on the west. These cities were taken from those which were given to the Levites. The Levites had no land-inheritance among their brethren since the Lord was their inheritance. But they were given cities to live in and fields to till so they could make a living. Out of the cities given to them, six were taken as cities of refuge.

These cities of refuge were set apart for those who might kill people unintentionally. If a person should intentionally kill another, then, according to the Law, it was "an eye for an eye, life for life." However, sometimes there were accidents. For instance, if a person were cutting a tree, and the axehead flew off the handle and killed someone, this was not done intentionally. Since it was unintentional, God said those people could flee to the cities of refuge before the avenger of blood caught up with them. When one fled into the city of refuge, then the assembly would judge between him and the avenger. If it was proven it was without intention, then his life was to be saved. He had to remain in the city of refuge until the high priest died. Then he could go back to his own inheritance. If he left the city of refuge before the high priest died and was met by the avenger of blood, he would be killed. So this was the ordinance of the Old Testament for a city of refuge (see Numbers 35).

Here the Psalmist says, "God is our refuge ..." In a sense, we are chased by our enemies, the world, Satan, sins, and our flesh. All of these try to devour us and defile us as virgins. As these forces surround us, they try to esnare us, tempt us, lead us astray and defile us. What can we do? We do not have the strength to resist these temptations nor the power to fight against the world and Satan. How can we keep our chastity before God? There is a way: flee to the city of refuge. Christ is our city of refuge, and as we flee to Him, we are safe, secure, and protected.

> ... and your life is hid with the Christ in God (Colossians 3:3).

So far as the redemptive work of Christ is concerned, we are in Him, and our life is hidden with Him. Because of that, we are protected, but, so far as our experience is concerned, sometimes we do not abide in Him.

Truth has two sides. We need to see that: (1) Christ has accomplished all things for us on Calvary's cross. This never changes because it is eternal. "But of Him are ye in Christ Jesus ..." and "... your life is hid with the Christ in God." This is our position, and here nothing can touch us. (2) Then there is the other side, which is our subjective experience. As far as this is concerned, there is always an "if." Positionally we are in Christ, but conditionally we can either abide in Him or not. Abiding simply means to "make a home." Sometimes we abide at home, and sometimes we wander. When we wander away from Christ, we lose protection. Temptations ensnare us, the world entices us and our enemy, Satan, attacks us. Therefore it is essential for us believers, as virgins, to abide in Christ, staying in the city of refuge. As long as we do this, we are preserved. This is the preservation of the saints.

In the Old Testament, the high priest would die because he was a human being, but in the New Testament, our High Priest never dies.

> Whence also he is able to save completely those who approach by him to God, always living to intercede for them (Hebrews 7:25).

Thank God we have a city of refuge and a High Priest who never dies. Therefore it behooves us that we never leave the city of refuge but stay there forever abiding in Christ. If we do this, we find we are saved from the hand of the enemy. It is in this way that we keep our virginity, our chastity towards the one Man Christ.

God is our refuge and strength

Notice that He is also our strength. In a sense, "refuge" is negative, keeping us safe and protecting us from evil; but, "strength" is positive. We not only can hide in Christ and be protected, but in Him and by Him, we have the strength to overcome our enemies. This is what we read in Romans 8:

> Who shall separate us from the love of Christ? tribulation or distress, or persecution, or famine, or nakedness, or danger, or sword? According as it is written, For thy sake we are put to death all the day long; we have been reckoned as sheep for

> slaughter. But in all these things we more than conquer through him that has love us (vv. 35-37).

It is true that in this world we have tribulation; but, the Lord said, "I have overcome the world" (John 16:33). So through Him who has loved us, we are more than conquerors.

Then notice this verse in II Corinthians 2:

> But thanks be to God, who always leads us in triumph in the Christ, and makes manifest the odour of his knowledge through us in every place (v. 14).

God always leads us in triumph in the Christ.

> I can do all things through Him who empowers me (Philippians 4:13).

Our Lord Jesus is not only our refuge where we can hide and be protected, but He is also our strength. And through Him who empowers us, we can do all things.

Of course, there is the need to learn the lesson that we can do nothing without Him (see John 15:5). As we try to do things and we are defeated many times, we will then learn this. But, it is only half the lesson. If we remain like this, we will become very passive, thinking that we can do nothing and therefore we do nothing. The other half of the lesson is, "I can do all things through Him who empowers me" because He is my strength (see Philippians 4:13).

... a help in distresses,
very readily found.

God has not promised us that we will go through this world without distresses, but He does promise to be a help in them.

A sister, Annie J. Flint, wrote a beautiful hymn and I will quote some of it for you.

God hath not promised skies always blue,
Flower-strewn pathways all our lives through;
God hath not promised sun without rain,
Joy without sorrow, peace without pain.

But God hath promised strength for the day,
Rest for the labor, light for the way,
Grace for the trials, help from above,
Unfailing sympathy, undying love.

She wrote, "God has not promised that the skies will always be blue, flowers strewn all the way of our lives, the sun without rain, joy without sorrow, or peace without pain."—He has not promised that we will have no problems or trials. "But He promises strength for the day"—not for tomorrow. "And He promises rest for the labor, light for the way, and grace for the trials."—He has said, "My grace is sufficient." "Help from above"— as our Psalm says, "a help in distresses." "Unfailing sympathy"—We have a High Priest who sympathizes with us. In Him we find "undying love."

In our Lord Jesus, help in distresses is very readily found. Whenever we need Him, He is there. He is truly our Friend. A friend in need is a friend indeed! This is the declaration of the virgins. In their lives, they have proved that "God is our refuge and strength, a help in distresses, very readily found."

Therefore will we not fear

Now they describe the tempest—what they have gone through:

> Therefore will we not fear though the earth be removed, and though the mountains be carried into the heart of the seas; Though the waters thereof roar and foam, though the mountains shake with the swelling thereof. Selah.

Even in the midst of all this turmoil, there is no need to fear because we know He is our refuge and strength. See how important it is that we go through these life experiences in order to learn to know Him as our refuge and strength. We will never learn to appreciate Him as our refuge and strength until we have gone through all these distresses. Therefore we thank God for all these things.

Part 2—The Secret (vv. 4-7)

Now the thought begins to change. From verse 4 to verse 7, it tells of a secret. Why is it when the sea is roaring, and the waves are rising, and the mountains are shaking that you can have such strength and peace? It says:

> There is a river the streams whereof make glad the city of God, the sanctuary of the habitations of the Most High.
>
> God is in the midst of her; she shall not be moved; God shall help her at the dawn of the morning.

What a contrast! Outside, the sea is foaming and roaring, but in the city, there is a river. If you are in the sea and it is foaming and roaring, it is a terrible thing. I don't know if you get seasick, but I do even when I think of going aboard a ship. Once when I was in England, we were to cross the English Channel in the morning to go to Switzerland for a conference. At breakfast that morning, when I thought of crossing the channel, I got cold sweats. I was so ashamed that I didn't dare tell anyone. After breakfast, I slipped out and went to a drug store and bought some pills for seasickness. After we got on the ship, it was so calm.

There was nothing to it, but as for me, I would get seasick whenever I would think of it.

The sea speaks of turbulence with roaring and foaming. The river speaks of a steady, quiet flow.

There is a river the streams
whereof make glad the city of God

Now, of course, this river runs from Genesis to Revelation. In Genesis, we see it after God planted the garden of Eden—He put a river there to water it. This river divided into four branches that literally covered the earth. This is that river of God.

Then when the children of Israel were in the wilderness, there was no water; but water came out of the smitten rock. That spiritual Rock and its "river" followed them all the way for forty years (see I Corinthians 10:4).

In Ezekiel 47, the prophet saw in a vision the Holy City and the temple. Out from the throne came a river. Its "waters issued out from under the threshold of the house eastward ... And the waters came down from under, from the right side of the house, south of the altar." The prophet began to measure it at a thousand cubits, and the water came to the ankles; another thousand cubits it came to the knees; another thousand cubits it came to the loins; another thousand cubits it was water to swim in. This water flowed into the Dead Sea and healed it. Also into the Dead Sea came all kinds of fish. And along where the water flowed, all kinds of trees came up. In other words, it is a river of life.

> ... but whosoever drinks of the water which I shall give him shall never thirst for ever, but the water which I shall give him shall become in him a fountain of water, springing up into eternal life (John 4:14).

In Revelation 22, you see the new Jerusalem, the Holy City. In it flows a river of life which comes from the throne of God and of the Lamb. Wherever this river of water flows, you find the tree of life in the middle of the waters as well as on the two sides. This speaks of the Spirit of life.

Now the metaphor changes. In the first stanza, we see God is our refuge—we are in Christ—and we learn to abide there to keep our chastity towards Hirn. In the second stanza, it is not only that we are in Christ, but it is also Christ in us. The river is in the city. Of course, this speaks collectively, but whether collectively or individually, it is the same. The virgins are like the city of God.

> There is a river the streams whereof make glad the city of God, the sanctuary of the habitations of the Most High.

Not only do we abide in Him, but He abides in us. If we abide in Him and He in us, then we bear much fruit.

We do give thanks that the Spirit of God is in us and the Spirit of God is that river of life. There is no end to its flow. It is never exhausted. How satisfying its water is! Here is the secret: The Spirit of life is in us individually and collectively, and because of that, Christ abides in us. As He abides in us, there is an inexhaustible supply of life. Life swallows up all death. It overcomes all things because it is resurrection life.

God is in the midst of her;
she shall not be moved

"If God be for us, who against us?" (Romans 8:31).

He is enough, and that life overcomes everything. That is why it says,

God shall help her
at the dawn of the morning.

It is true that He allows even the dark night to come. Sometimes we have to go through experiences that are like death. Out of death comes resurrection. The night is far gone, and the dawn is coming (see Romans 13:12). The dawn speaks of resurrection. This is the secret to overcoming everything.

Part 3—The Calm of Victory (vv. 8-11)

> Come, behold the works of Jehovah, what desolations he hath made in the earth: He hath made wars to cease unto the end of the earth; he breaketh the bow, and cutteth the spear in sunder; he burneth the chariots in the fire.
>
> Be still, and know that I am God ...

When we are in the tempest, we learn the secret of the abiding Spirit of life in us. As we learn this, we enter into stillness. "Be still, and know that I am God." Whenever temptations, distresses, or problems come, we tend to go out and fight against all of them because we know they are trying to lead us away from Christ. As we fight, trying to keep our chastity towards God, we are strained and distressed, and there is much unrest within us. We soon find out we are no match. We fail. When the tempest is raging outside, we are raging within.

It is only as we learn the secret of hiding in Christ that we begin to draw upon the river of life within us. Then our striving and struggling will cease, and we will rest in faith. We will be still and watch God work it out. God is God, and He is well able not only to cope with but also to overcome all these situations. If we will be still and watch Him, He will get glory out of these problems.

> For thus saith the Lord Jehovah, the Holy One of Israel: In returning and rest shall ye be saved, in quietness and confidence shall be your strength (Isaiah 30:15).

By returning and resting, we shall be saved, in quietness and confidence. We have perfect confidence in God; He is our refuge; He is our strength, and because He is, we shall overcome!

Jehovah of hosts is with us;
the God of Jacob is our high fortress.
Selah.

We are told this story about John Wesley when he was dying: He was very weak and didn't have the strength to speak. He tried but could not. Finally, it seemed as if he gathered up all his strength and said, "The best of all is, God is with us." Then after a while, he raised his hand and shouted, "The best of all, God is with us." Then he passed on.

This sums up the life of John Wesley. And dear brothers and sisters, we must remember, God is with us! We are in Him; He is in us. Nothing can separate us … nothing! If God is with us, who can be against us? If we commit ourselves to His keeping, He is well able to keep us.

Do we flee to the city of refuge? Do we draw upon His inexhaustible resource of resurrection life? If we do, then we will find He will keep us blameless and pure until the day of Christ (see Philippians 1:6, 10; I Corinthians 1:8). The "day of Christ" means at the time when we shall appear before Him at the judgment seat. We cannot keep ourselves, but He can. As we believe Him and trust Him, we find He is fully committed to our keeping. May the Lord help us as we walk through this life.

TITLES AVAILABLE
from Christian Fellowship Publishers
By Watchman Nee

Aids to "Revelation"
Amazing Grace
Back to the Cross
A Balanced Christian Life
The Better Covenant
The Body of Christ: A Reality
The Character of God's Workman
Christ the Sum of All Spiritual Things
The Church and the Work – 3 Vols
The Church in the Eternal Purpose of God
"Come, Lord Jesus"
The Communion of the Holy Spirit
The Finest of the Wheat – Vol. 1
The Finest of the Wheat – Vol. 2
From Faith to Faith
From Glory to Glory
Full of Grace and Truth – Vol. 1
Full of Grace and Truth – Vol. 2
Gleanings in the Fields of Boaz
The Glory of His Life
God's Plan and the Overcomers
God's Work
Gospel Dialogue
Grace Abounding
Grace for Grace
Heart to Heart Talks
Interpreting Matthew
Journeying towards the Spiritual
The King and the Kingdom of Heaven
The Latent Power of the Soul
Let Us Pray
The Life That Wins
The Lord My Portion
The Messenger of the Cross
The Ministry of God's Word
My Spiritual Journey
The Mystery of Creation
Powerful According to God
Practical Issues of This Life
The Prayer Ministry of the Church
The Release of the Spirit
Revive Thy Work
The Salvation of the Soul
The Secret of Christian Living
Serve in Spirit
The Spirit of Judgment
The Spirit of the Gospel
The Spirit of Wisdom and Revelation
Spiritual Authority
Spiritual Discernment
Spiritual Exercise
Spiritual Knowledge
The Spiritual Man
Spiritual Reality or Obsession
Take Heed
The Testimony of God
The Universal Priesthood of Believers
Whom Shall I Send?
The Word of the Cross
Worship God
Ye Search the Scriptures

The Basic Lesson Series

Vol. 1 - A Living Sacrifice
Vol. 2 - The Good Confession
Vol. 3 - Assembling Together
Vol. 4 - Not I, But Christ
Vol. 5 - Do All to the Glory of God
Vol. 6 - Love One Another

TITLES AVAILABLE
from Christian Fellowship Publishers
By Stephen Kaung

Abiding in God
Acts
"But We See Jesus"—*the Life of the Lord Jesus*
Discipled to Christ—*As Seen in the Life of Simon Peter*
God's Purpose for the Family
Government and Ministry in the Local Church
The Gymnasium of Christ
Isaiah
In the Footsteps of Christ
The Key to "Revelation" – Vol. 1
The Key to "Revelation" – Vol. 2
The Master's Training
Ministering the Word of God
Moses, the Servant of God
Nehemiah
New Covenant Living & Ministry
Now We See the Church—*the Life of the Church, the Body of Christ*
Proverbs
Shepherding
The Songs of Degrees—*Meditations on Fifteen Psalms*
The Splendor of His Ways—*Seeing the Lord's End in Job*
Titus
Worship

The "God Has Spoken" Series
Seeing Christ in the Old Testament, Part One
Seeing Christ in the Old Testament, Part Two
Seeing Christ in the New Testament